AT MY DOOR

ARCANUM POETICA

DARSHIT PANDIT

Contents

1. Ode to a Doll

With eyes and lips of an innocent child
How many fancies have you beguiled?
How the strength of an unmoving stare you muster
Soft hair dangling down like fairy-duster
Rosy cheeks and strawberry lips
Chiselled and polished fingertips
Quiet confidante with a gaze of unrest
At children's tea, you are the most welcomed guest
Dressed up in silken, woollen dresses
In gracious plumes, in greying tresses
With the mien of a hummingbird sitting still
With the placidity of a snow-capped hill
You lay beside children as they rest
They work at your unspoken behest
Every answer unknown dwell in your eyes
Your unmoving lips can never tell lies
Like the soul of a frozen fairy child
In your delicate bosom, lives a secret wild
A longing to more than cherish
All those children who shall one day perish
The laughter in their mother-kissed cheeks
Quenching of wonders which their soul seeks
Your dresses still smell of ginger tea

Of the biscuits slathered in honey
What goes inside your porcelain head
Does it wonder about the unsaid
What do you think while you wake at night
What do you ponder, with still sight
While children snuggle you in their blanket
Do you think of their honied tete-a-tete
What mysterious force compels you to live
Your enigmatic smile, what secret does it give
Speak aloud doll, I implore
You never get the dress you yesterday wore
What are the shadows your smiles often cast
What lies in your unnerving stillness vast
Whilst you sit in a posture demure
What secret does, your smile, ensure
Queen of mannequins, tell me true
Which poison does your clever mind brew
What do you whisper in children's ears
How do you charm their dried tears
What does the scent of tea, in you, evoke
What do you make of unknown candle smoke
While under the pretence of thinking at night
While you stare into the candlelight
What goes on in your porcelain head
Tell me what lays on your lips red
With bright eyes and innocent smiles
What are your diabolic wiles

That tempts children into drinking tea
What during night hours, can you see
What did you make of candle smoke
Before you fell and you broke

2. Jewel

Wrought by bearded Ironmaster
A jewel begat of disaster
Set inside a ring of gold
Inscribed upon by word untold
Passed upon by bearers of bloodline
Sworn upon by Mnemosyne
Brought ashore by raging tempest
By waves crashing upon the coast of West
Dropped into the sea by unfortunate bearer
Who had held life none the dearer
Whose bleeding hands coronated the curse
Cease laughter, for dissonance worse
It lay by the unmerciful shore
With cold countenance, by fate's door
In the hands of unfortunate sailors
Held by the scarlet stained sea-hailers
Past the eyes of buried knights
Looked upon by moonlit nights
Under blest vestments worn
Trembling in the cries of mourn
By the Eucharist's intoxicating brew
Revelling in a tattoo on the pew
With a burning ecstasy of ungodly vice

Sired by the brimming chalice
Under sword of steel and silver armour
Under stolen whispers and hidden amour
By the cup quaffed and secrets unravelled
By the midnight hour in moonlight dappled
The ring slit and severed with heart of stone
Until by blood, it mounted the throne
Crests with unfaithful legions abound
The gold-set jewel continued to hound
The bearer with misery, oh misery eternal
With a burning rapture, a rapture infernal
Until the wearer implored the grave
With cries, with a lunatic's rave
One by one, the lineage forsaken
To their coffins, were shrouded and taken
Until the stone, the ethereal jewel
The gold-set stone, the ornament cruel
Was cast into the fires of which it was born
By a gaunt man of town forlorn
But as it embraced its grave and cradle
The flames began to slowly swaddle
The ring in hues of burning flame
The gaunt man was never quite the same
His face gave into the madness of nil
Bearing the ring, he stood still

3. Walks She

If you were blessed enough to tread

The mansion of the dead

Where the flames are shackled to the wicks

The air with dread, with paddles of Styx

Past the counting room and the forlorn tea

With tufted footsteps, walks she

She shuffles the deck of painted cards

Bestrewing them upon scarlet shards

And the clinking of the lantern sounds absurd

It is the only sound that can be heard

The nightingales are immersed in soliloquy

With muffled footsteps, walks she

The empty wine glass with temper of caprice

Of likeness to her heart, full of malice

They spurned to gaze at her, the mirrors

And if you were ever blessed to sight those horrors

The horrors of mansion from where you can never flee

With swift and silenced footsteps, walks she

The footsteps liberate the beating of my heart

In a fearful symphony that sets us apart

She- shall walk upon the carpet

She- shall crawl into the casket

Where the earth shall tremble from beneath your knee

With smothered footsteps, walks she
The horse carriages she once rode
Her silken apparel pressed in woad
Making obeisance to fealty that never existed
But her, to keep walking, her conscience insisted
And she still walks, beneath the forsaken pine tree
With dull footsteps, walks she
Clad in the white veil she stood
In the carriage crafted of wood
For her sepulchre had already been wrought
In the ghastly, undying, vice of besot
And she could, she did foresee
How with deadened footsteps, walks she
With wreath of holly upon her head
She walked, oh she did tread
The unending trail of thorns
On the Devil's unmerciful horns
She did walk, she did bury
With those ominous footsteps, walks she
And today with lantern, she is about to saunter
To turn her back on the pasts that haunt her
Under the very pine tree where the carriage did halt
Too far away from the church's archivolt
Condemned to the unsaid decree
With shrouded footsteps, walks she
She- shall be the one who lifts the candle
She- shall be the one who plays the gamble

For it is in her blood, it is in her breath
She holds the ashes of the wreath
She walks like a vulture, at last, set free
With footsteps approaching me, walks she

4. Tea

While I lay fairly sober in my bed
Immersed in the tomes of the dead
Under a candle as it dripped tallow
And as in those mysteries I prepared to wallow
I felt a tap at the windowpane
A wanderer of night, with the guise of Cain
Compelled by the curious affair
At the moonlight, I ceased to stare
And climbing out of my blankets warm
Leaving behind the leather-bound tome
I sauntered into the night dreary
With bleary eyes and face weary
The stove came alive, enkindled
The end of my spine tingled
The kettle began to steam and boil
As though going through strife and turmoil
And in the smoke, which bore semblance to a veil
I could see, but never feel
A faceless mass, with two eyes
Two crafty gossamers, woven of lies
That stared at me with venom penetrating
That a thousand souls would never be close to sating
With my eyes relentlessly clashing

Into the night air, slowly crashing
Methought my sobriety mustn't be true
Perhaps I had drunk a forgotten brew
That was making me dream, oh dream
And I could see in the steam
Those two unyielding, inexorable eyes
That gleamed like paralyzed fireflies
Deigning to make those eyes disappear
To banish away my savage fear
I poured tea in a cup and kept it on the table
Suddenly it went according to the fable
Where men and women at night convened
Around the corners of my house, they careened
The moonlight beaming at the apple-red tea
Steam still curled around it like serpent of the tree
It was the tempter's brew
Towards itself it drew
My fancy, being the most enthralled human being
Who was blessed with seeing
Tempter or tempest I knew not
The one which sought to slake my drought
With a felicity sinister
Begat of Satrina or Gorgon's sister
Fathoming none the more of the beverage
Or of the wanderer knocking the window ledge
And with the nepenthe in masquerade
Venom, pure venom they trade

With burning sage in guise

They make a bargain of vice

With the lies of Seraphim's herald, the devils of hells

Brought along the Devil's bells

With feral spirit and pomp

Past the boat of Psychopomp

They knocked my door

Divulging all the mysteries of lore

They stood nearby my bed

For it was tea- with the dead

5. Lady of Lore

Once lived a girl, no near, no farther
Born of mother, never knew her father
Came into existence, by word of Gospel
Or perhaps from the crevices of Hell
But came she, and tolled the bells of the Church
Beneath the spiny tree of birch
As if in the shed of Bethlehem with heaven above
Blessed by the wings of the snow-white dove
Crying, cooing, and bringing thunder
Whilst every nun and priest stood in wonder
Whether she was sent and staked on trial
Or sent by the ram-faced Belial
But as the scarlet stained child wept
Her mother, for once and forever slept
In a pool of her own blood, she lay
The baby cried, swathed in blankets grey
With branded behind her eyes
She cried and quaffed her life of lies
No frail answer ever sufficed
Was she truly the vessel of Christ
Or was she some malefic being undaunted
By unforgettable past, haunted
Defying and defying every edict

Scorned at by the Benedict
In the name of heresy, stake her
Let her fall in slumber, never wake her
Authoring word of Eve's crime eternal
The fall of the Host infernal
As an aureate leaf, while the Church went berserk
She preserved forever the memorial of her work
Past her summer years she sauntered on autumn's periphery
Revered and worshiped by the women of the nunnery
She fell ill, bearing the countenance of Christ himself
As two treatises piled on the bookshelf
They prayed for her, mourned, for resurrection was nevermore
For the saintly, hallowed, lady of Lore
And she died, of mysterious cause
No Transfiguration for this loss
Her faced mummified, spurned at by Anubis
While the vestment-clad ones called it the holy Genesis
Cross struck upon her head
Blood beside the dead
Stored in a glass vial
Was her eternal trial
Her face a Sarcophagus still, bereft of gold
And they saw her in wonder, the horror did unfold
For she, was no longer alone
Conjured up with life, by forces unknown
And her eyes, never flitting
She is still sitting

With a fragment of her life's love
In the lingering air of the dove
Her gaunt face and wide-open eyes
Defy all the gossamers of lies
And the Seraphim that looked at her while she
Lost the light of her eyes underneath the birch tree
Must have branded upon her face
The sigil of his most kind grace
For she, with face of stillborn
Has never once, celebrated her mourn

6. Smoke

The divine comedy of an infernal herald
In air and dust, pensively dappled
The prelude of prayers by men and saint
Of engulfing, every tarnish and taint
As fire's eclipsed purfle, to never remember
Like sweven seen in dying ember
Burn the shackles, the dead abound
Drifting on the waters of Styx and hound
Engulfing the eyes of Stata Mater
In the Celt's devilish barter
The cruel and divine satire
In mockery of fire
Serpent of Devil, dwelling in air
With mien like kohl on face fair
Sojourning in Church and hell
As censer burning bellow the bell
Reigning the chariots of legions infernal
With Prometheus's fire, unknelled, eternal
Wafting and dying into the night
Redolent of death, an ephemeral sight
Into an ineffable, fathomless, form
Subjugated to no worldly norm
Maugre the worldly norms, it goes to drift

In an ethereal, surreal rift
A divine comedy- indeed
A tragic being clad in funeral weed
A steed to Valhalla, hailed of divine
A Pope's first hallowed wine
Cast forever into the penumbra, unseen
At the sight where necromancers convene
Glory of smoke and glory of fire
Both belonging to the same sire
One, the feeble masquerade
The other, blazing, never to fade
Consuming everything unburnt
As if the perfidy of being were already learnt
The dock of the unsaid
Sauntering onto the land of dead
Acquitting the lamenters and ferry
Amidst the intoxicating sherry
Of smoke; drifting once again through the bars
Above, beyond the glaring stars
Oh- smoke, the mystifying censer
Making the air thick and denser
Reigning above the grave headstones
Above the cracking prophetical bones
Abound the long dead graves of mire
And ode to smoke, certainly not to fire

7. Legion

ond wine
Walking into herd of loitering swine
With impious mien they tread upon ashes
Insanity, lunatic laughter, and devilish lashes
In haunting tomb, house of the dead
Shattering every shackle on his feet or head
He- with hordes and legions of devils
In the rich, and the unholy revels
Slashing himself, with stones, blood on his breast
Sealing covenant in flesh, on Lucifer's behest
With myriad of men whispering and chanting
Into madness, into eternal void granting
Potestates and conjurors in the follow
Unto the abyss and hollow
Trembling in front of the of calvary's wrath
Where once diabolic reign hath
Tempted by tempest and night infernal
Into abyss and void eternal
Upon wings of dragon and beating drums
Where the serpent hisses and the trumpet hums
In his lead follows the fair men clashing cymbals
Clad in lamen with sigils and symbols
They march, unto death and soul of man's censer

In the follow of the tempter
He leads- a Legion, he leads an army infernal
A military of sins eternal
And commands them, subjugating man to hell
Like Lucifer who from Heaven fell
Unto their flesh, blood, and soul
And curious affairs of singing dole
Thy covenant shall be sealed- earner of His ire
Cast the scapular into the fire
And woe betide the infidel
Those who in the lead, and fell
Into abyss, Tartarus, be never born
Your burning crest shall be forlorn
And for every drop of blood that fell
A thousand of them banished to Hell
With scarred Lamen and mauled skin
Slain, the demon's begat and kin
And HE- said from above
By flesh and feather of my dove
Leave him, by behest of Lord
Tremble before the Blest Knight's sword
Shiver before the Pontius
For he never ceases to see us
Begone, fiend, into herd of swine
Never show again your cursed mien
And the Legion, branding the herd
Without leaving behind a Devil or bird

They drowned; their corpses devoured by nether
Drifting with dromedary, into ether
Leaving behind no crest in their wake
No sign of blood on the burning-stake

8. Yule Night

A night of Yule, an ephemeral revel
A night sired by the Devil
With men and women with ghostly mien
Conjured and crafted by play divine
Leaving behind the evocation caskets
They trod upon the embroidered carpets
Dancing, with madness, they convened
From one corner to other they careened
In mockery of sanity
Exhibition of vanity
But, ah, it was pride that he did fall
And he reigns in ether, as they dance in this Ball
With countenance cold
They never cease to uphold
Clad in gossamers of arachnid's crafter
Drowning the hall in dervish laughter
Drinking some ethereal beverage from skulls
Fashioning on the walls, broken hulls
The hulls that had been shattered by tempest of devil
That now stood on the walls of the hall of revel
The air with laughter and diabolic smiles
With twisted words and perfidious wiles
Seemed to baffle the mind, and bemuse the head

And sire up against words unsaid
Through the night, continued the dance
Somewhere from glove, it turned to lance
By the scimitar, by the drink, there was no still soul
For they had been consumed, one and whole
And for every step they trod, for every step feral
Every moment they spent of the night ephemeral
Condemned them, bargained their existence divine
Traded them by every sip of wine
And the deck of cards bestrewn
On the shrouds impeccably sewn
Were no less than life gone
Reduced to a cursed, ghastly, moan
The night of Yule, was no night of mirth
But a terrible bargain's birth
Where every second of tumult
Every member of coven or cult
Where every morsel consumed in dine
Where every sip consumed of wine
Where the countenance of the curse divine
Where the revellers ghostly mien
Was forever captured
There maddening fancies forever enraptured
They danced themselves to insanity and death
But resurrected for eternity by the covenant's wreath
They danced
They laughed as the night advanced

But they never took off the dress made by the long-legged
crafter
And never did end the maddening laughter
Their legs turning to nothing but bone
To ghostly and never-ending moan
Never did the farewell send
For never did the night end

9. Gold

The bells toll'd at the hour of lament
Sang the crooked tree's tenant
I stood in front of a graveyard
As a sauntering, stranded bard
Facing the deathbeds of men and women
Hailing from valley, moor, and glen
Somebody tapped at their coffin's door
As though assuming a creature of lore
And divulged none their words stern
Of their design, I couldn't learn
Surely an attire of my own mind's craft
Was shrouding the sail of my sanity's raft
I turned back, my heart burning with fears feral
As prophesied the seers a fate visceral
The Sarcophagus, with its eyes gleaming
Like a corpse, in ether, dreaming
With the beautiful and terrible mien
Of a pensiveness almost divine
And the Sarcophagus never lifting an eye
Bones and blood of wheat and rye
Had scarcely turned to dust
And with the countenance of a bust
And without ever uttering a sentence

The sarcophagus made acquaintance
With terror in my heart, exclaimed I
Did my sight, me, just defy?
For such was the penumbra of the being
Casting into shadows, what I was seeing
By apprehension and deceitful wiles
I was ushered into crooked smiles
And before I could implore
Or draw a blessed dagger of yore
I stopped dead in my track
Blinded by the night's black
For the sarcophagus was staring
His golden garment wearing
I screamed again, having seen
To swerve aside the entity, before I could deign
Surging through my veins the blood
With terror began to flood
As if he who in caskets dwelt
Had made his stern decorum felt
And once again screamed I
Was I living an unsaid lie?
No sooner than later, the coffin crumbled to dust
The silver and gold turned to mere rust
But he still lived, weeping the tears
That had been ice, as cold as his fears
The golden attire, that lied as rubble
Was Avon's bane, doubled double

And stood as bold as urn of brass
Like an invisible, unsheathed cutlass
He lived, in the floundering raft
But he was certainly not my craft
All hail, tolling bell
A dying flame, fallen from Hell
His black wings were engulfed in fire
The Sarcophagus, had earnt ire
Still denying to give up life
As though vowed to eternal strife
"Knave of man or Devil," cried I
The wisp of smoke was now a sigh
And as the unmerciful reverie broke
The pyre slowly turned to smoke
Crushed into ruin was the golden bust
Forever turned into dust

10. Tomb of Time

A mausoleum of time and dead
Filled with inexplicable dread
Undisturbed- by the trite skirmishes of this world
Unbeknownst to all those pages of history unfurled
Where time, like a person carrying malady unknown
By the hovering nihilism forlorn
Bows, by the tomb, pays obeisance
To the ashes, casts a heedful glance
Sits beside the sepulchre, little relevance bearing
The footsteps no longer hearing
Falls he, and mourns his funeral in a pool of blood
Mixes into the earth and mud
Prophetical bones, ledgers of seers
Tomes of the crown's greatest fears
Lie, with incredible comedy of all divine
Rebuke every word of Mnemosyne
For no nemesis ever trod upon the grave
Or left behind the forsaken cave
No restless, careless, uncertainty
Ever stood the test of sanity
And the tomb, haunted by its own wall
Inscribed with tales of its own fall
Stood still- with no battle ever fathomed alive

But of peace they never ceased to deprive
There is no parting of ways
Does what he thinks is what he says?
For no tomb, that ever stood so still
Stood against, time's will
For ever and ever, in infallible reign
Living in its own bane
This, is the mausoleum of time
The grave of every past crime
That is at war with itself, with its own master
Pursued by destruction, faster and faster
Nearly touching its own shadow, its own pain
But escaping, abdicating its own reign
It carries its own body in this land
And bears his own brand
Treads this forsaken grave of time
And sleeps in this tomb of time
But does the tomb dwell in the cave alone
Or is this not, in time, lone
Perhaps if you were to walk
To pluck away a sleeping stalk
Throwing it on the grave with thought
Perhaps the deaths wouldn't be for naught
But the stalk wilts away and dries
Like all those echoing cries
This, is the tomb of time, and will never cease to be
Come may the worst storm of the sea

Come may the fall of crowns and thrones
Turn may every person to bones
But this is the bearer of its own crime
This, is the tomb of time

11. Letter

Thunder struck and the forest shook
Trees fell on the path near the brook
Clad in clothes, drenched and damp
Rain drops killing the flame of the lamp
Plunging the world into nightly fears
But no rain was greater than her tears
No- the hill could never be reached by night
A couple of hours and she would be out of sight
Devoured by some beast formidable
Her death proclaimed by priest credible
And the truth, the truth would be buried in her own grave
The path of oblivion, her funeral would pave
This was but as tragic as life would be
The day of light she would never see
But someone, anyone, needed to know
If only a miracle, would itself, bestow
But this was not a tale of lore
This was life, not a story of yore
Grabbing scroll from the depths of her vestments
As though authoring in her last testaments
Damp, more by tears than by rain
She wandered for light, like the soul of Cain
And writing under moon's light

She wrote away her last night
And as the hour came near
She abandoned every fear
This, was no new tale
And every blowing gale
Killed her, filled her with misery and mourn
Until the vultures came alone
But the letter
For worse or better
Lay close to her skin, sewn
Stared at by the glaring moon
And the vultures, with contempt, refused to peck
At the brittle and sour sheet sewn to her neck
Everyone came and went by
Believing in the lie
The terror of her life
To negate which she bore the strife
That took her life
Like a venomous knife
And the letter, sat at the top of the hill
And there is sits still
Its countenance, and that of others
Shell shocked sisters and brothers
Never ceased to stare for the better
At the bearer of the truth, the letter
But what did she write, as she sat dying
What was lie she feared, as she sat crying

Remains a mystery
And the rest is history
How everything changed for worse or better
All because of that one letter

12. Shrouds

The old hag dwelt outside the village

Carrying only one painted image

Of a man, unknown, never seen by any soul

Save those eyes of hers, lined by kohl

She sewd shrouds of people, on one old loom

Near the tree where the shrubs bloom

Shuttle going back and forth, weaving

No silken thread leaving

Elaborate patterns, impeccable patterns

Clad in those old tatters

She wove the garment of the dead

And clothed them upon their deathbed

With lamp at night and sight at day

No soul had ever heard her say

Never an affair apart from the clothes of the dead

Ever seemed to wander in her wrinkled head

What made her spin and weave and seam

When did she ever blaspheme?

That this silken business befell her

No one ever dared to tell her

That a world there was, outide the loom

Outside the dock of despair and doom

So she weaved her life away and death

And they wrapped her in her own cloth, like a sheath

The dreadful tapestry lies their still

No robin flies about to sing in a trill

But still remains, untouched the image

Which once was owned, by the hag of the village

The beldam had sighted the fair man once

And, as they said, she still hunts

Weaving their hearts into the cloth

Where flesh and fabric made a troth

That was how lustre adorned the attire

And as she lay in the Yard, in her own satire

Her heart beating, never still

And the cloth, her spoil of cult, her kill

Enveloped her whole being

And although she would never be seeing

Her mockery of hearts

Of the diabolic arts

That compelled her to weave, to weave her life away

To cease seeing ever, the light of day

13. Quietude

They all talked of the dead

All the words which must be unsaid

And as a dark silence befell

Like a serpent striking from Hell

Struck by infernal demilance

They all fell into silence

They mocked the dead and played their cards

Assuming to be Epirus's bards

They used the planchette and spelt words

They pretented to incant and staked birds

But now people bring them flowers in baskets

For they earnt the ire of the dwellers of caskets

And I- walking to the graveyard

Gathering every cursed card

My bare legs brushing against the thorny roots

Snow crunching under my boots

The path, redolent of forgottems dreams

Of shrouds and silken seams

Carrying candelabra in my hand

Trembling, my tongue tasting bland

My footsteps accompanied by whispers

Something brushed against my leg; whiskers

A fairly uninterested black cat, yowling

Scampering off into the woods, howling
And stood in front of me, the dead
With sewn eyes and severed head
Bearing little semblance to their headstones
As though composed of merely bones
They talked, saying words with no fathom
In their strange fashion
For the curious affair
And the haunted air
Had turned my senses to nil
Slowly corrupting with deceitful will
Until it thrilled me and I reveled
And my own headstone, I bevelled
And the dead, with plain mien
Near the crooked tree of pine
Lay- they were my kin
And swen to their skin
Were those cards, the curse
Their final destination, their hearse
Madly, I sauntered ahead
Tears and blood, I bled
They were gone- it was my doing
And as the wind was blowing
I cast the cards into fire, let them burn
And what I did learn
Was to turn my back on the feud
Respect the quietude

To bow to the hellish demilance
To never break the silence
And all this brings one line to my head
Never, ever, speak of the dead

14. Cestrum Nocturnum

Drifting through the open ledge

Past the thickets and the hedge

Like intoxicating censer

Making the air denser

Seeping into the nostrils, piercing the nightly air

Muddling every thought fair

Like a fairy's clever pastime

More deceitful than the last time

Constantly befogs and bemuses

Every one of the mind's muses

Tantalizing, like the scent of poisonberry

Making every fancy merry

A play of the airy folk

A perfume stored in jar of oak

The ink of letters on acorn written

The scent splashed on Greek chiton

Drifitng, wafting through the air, careless

And as you breath it, it left you airless

Made from the elixir of flowers

Or sweet wine fermented for hours

Perhaps it is the musk in forest found

With no periphery or bound

It never ceases to drift, to bemuse and muddle

To baffle the mind, to play and befuddle

15. At my Door

A haunting month of December
The perfect hour to dismember
Every ungracious plume of past
To aside, the scythe, cast
And as Uranus had fallen when his sons did thwart
That had fallen from my churning heart
It was an ember, the seed of an undying fire
Every unworthy fancy that had earnt my ire
That now filled my bosom with every thought unwonted
And I stood there, like cavalry, undaunted
Roll, oh tempest, beguile the abyss, make it rise
Flood the towns and bourgs with fiery vice
Standing by the dock of every boat that had ever sailed
Where Sparta and Troy had all once hailed
There stood I, by the crashing shores
As the vengeance ebbed, so did the sea's roars
But a scent in its wake; a shadow, lingered
The peaceful beating of my heart it hindered
And my every footfall it pursued without rest
As though it were bearing the Plutonian crest
Until I reached my formidable door
And to forsake my countenance, I did implore
But while I had silenced the fire burning into my core

It had pursued me from the shore
A grey cloud that spurned to thunder
What was it, I did wonder
For I was sure at what I had seen
When by the mirror I had been
Staring at its face deceitful
With unwelcome face unnervingly heedful
It was not me, a doppelganger unknown
The crows cawed in a nightly moan
The waning moon glaring with unmerciful sight
I breathed with terror, in the middle of night
Terror, fear, Pandemonium without footstep crept
And in the midst, a wailful being wept
Lamenting with tears, with burning tears
Astounding me with fantastic fears
And I stood, with manner unknown to date
But I did with frigid heart wait
Until it ebbed into Tartarus dark
Until it was all no longer stark
With no corporeal form
With no rule or norm
It stood there, and all its eyes upon me dwelt
Such terror never had I felt
And creeping into my very clenched heart
The current of my vein, the upstart
And then the air, tinged with scent
A change of atmosphere, it underwent

And she, clad in silken dress, at me stared
With the eyes of Cerberus, at me, she glared
With dagger in her hand and crooked smile on her face
She stroked her scarlet dress's lace
Twirling a lock of kohl-black hair
She never stopped to unceasingly stare
With ineffable iridescence she did appear
With eyes that did inexplicably endear
She held the knife, her knuckles whitened
Her grip on the dagger, slowly tightened
And smashing headfirst into the mirror she fell
Smoke, she was, from the pits of hell
No existence had they bore
No crest did they wore
But the knife that somehow remained in this realm professed
By me it was for now, and forever possessed
Astonishingly, the pages of lore
Do not turn their back on our door
For the minstrels who weave our fate
Must haven't sought sate
In this trite fable, in this short occurrence bleak
A comedy of my fate, by treason of destiny, they must seek
So, I left behind the cursed attire
And I approached the dock where dwelt the fire
Where my fate was struck by thunder
Where I had been baffled with terrifying wonder
Where I sought the epiphanous morrow

Where ran the waters of sorrow
As I sighted the clear water
They saw, for they sought her
The one who had perished at my house
Who had slipped into endless drowse
Her, they wanted, the only one they could see
The one that had passed her curse to me
And once more, the tempest hails
Knocking the masts and sails
Headstones emerge from sandy coasts
Arrive from nether, the unseen hosts
For the Host is no longer here
And the surrogate is rare
The wearer of the dress had held
The curse no dearer; she wasn't unknelled
For by the perfidy of the soul gaunt
That still continues to haunt
Me to my bosom's core
It was the one who betrayed me to the shore
And now they look, with unwavering stare
No longer the crest of any Legion they bear
Convulsed with grief, stricken with fear
The crashing of waves, I distinctly hear
And the forgotten plumes for nether
Forget me in ether